MN

LIFE CYCLES

The Green Turtle

Diana Noonan

CHELSEA CLUBHOUSE

An Imprint of Chelsea House Publishers
A Haights Cross Communications Company

Philadelphia

This edition first published in 2003 in the United States of America by Chelsea Clubhouse, a division of Chelsea House Publishers and a subsidiary of Haights Cross Communications.

Chelsea Clubhouse
1974 Sproul Road, Suite 400
Broomall, PA 19008-0914

The Chelsea House world wide web address is www.chelseahouse.com

Library of Congress Cataloging-in-Publication Data

Noonan, Diana.
  The green turtle / by Diana Noonan.
  p. cm. — (Life cycles)
  Summary: An introduction to the physical characteristics, behavior, and development from egg to adult of the green turtle, a reptile that is endangered.
  ISBN 0-7910-6967-2
  1. Green turtle—Life cycles—Juvenile literature. [1. Green turtle.
  2. Turtles. 3. Endangered species.] I. Title. II. Series.
  QL666.C536 N66 2003
  597.92'8—dc21

                                                                    2002000032

First published in 1999 by
MACMILLAN EDUCATION AUSTRALIA PTY LTD
627 Chapel Street, South Yarra, Australia, 3141

Copyright © Diana Noonan 1999
Copyright in photographs © individual photographers as credited

Edited by Anne McKenna
Text design by Polar Design
Cover design by Linda Forss

Printed in China

Acknowledgements
Cover: A green sea turtle. (Australian Picture Library/Pacific Stock)

A.N.T. Photo Library, pp. 4 © David Paton, 5 © B. G. Thomson, 6, 8, 12, 17 & 30, 20, 21 & 30, 22, 25, 26, 27 © Kelvin Aitken, 7, 15, 19, 24 © Ron & Valerie Taylor, 10, 13 & 30, 14 © Bill Bachman, 16 © David B. Carter, 18 © Mike Thomas, 23 & 30 © Martin Harvey; 28 & 30 © Norbert Wu; Auscape, p. 11 © D. Parer & E. Parer-Cook.

While every care has been taken to trace and acknowledge copyright, the publisher tenders their apologies for any accidental infringement where copyright has proved untraceable.

Contents

Life Cycles

All animals change as they live and grow. They begin life as tiny creatures. They become adults that will produce their own young. The green turtle has its own special life cycle.

Most turtles live on land and in fresh water.
The green turtle belongs to the sea turtle
family. It lives in the ocean.

Turtles Are Reptiles

Turtles belong to a group of animals called reptiles. Reptiles are cold-blooded animals. They are as cold or as warm as the air or water around them.

beak

shell

scales

flipper

Small pieces of hard skin called scales cover a reptile's body. The green turtle's head, **flippers**, and belly have leathery scales. A shell protects the green turtle's belly and back. Hard, bony scales called **scutes** cover the shell.

Protection

The green turtle's shell covers most of its body. But the green turtle cannot pull its head and flippers into the shell. It depends on its large size and speed in the water for protection.

An adult turtle may reach more than 3 feet (1 meter) long and weigh 400 pounds (180 kilograms) or more. It can swim more than 18 miles per hour (30 kilometers per hour).

Swimming

The green turtle has a flat body to help it move easily through ocean waters. Its front flippers are shaped like wide paddles. The green turtle uses these flippers to pull itself through the water. It uses its back flippers like **rudders** to steer.

Breeding

Green turtles are ready to **breed** when they are between 20 and 50 years old. They breed every two or three years.

Migration

Green turtles **migrate** to the beach where they hatched. They often must swim long distances.

Mating

Hundreds of turtles migrate to the same place to find a partner. They **mate** in water close to the beach.

These two green turtles are mating.

Leaving the Water

The female is ready to lay her eggs a few weeks after mating. She leaves the water and goes ashore at night.

This female green turtle goes ashore to lay her eggs.

The female's legs are not strong enough to lift her heavy body off the beach. She uses her strong flippers to pull herself across the sand.

The Nesting Place

The female finds a nesting place that the high tides cannot reach. She uses her flippers to scrape a wide hollow in the sand.

Laying Eggs

The female uses her back flippers to dig a deep hole. She lays a **clutch** of about 100 eggs in the hole.

This female is laying her eggs.

Eggs

The eggs are white. The shells are soft and leathery to keep them from breaking as they fall into the hole. The female covers the eggs with sand.

The female will cover these eggs with sand.

A female leaves the beach after laying her eggs.

The female returns to the sea before sunrise. Green turtles may lay eggs two or three times on the same beach in one breeding season.

Incubation

The warmth of the sand helps to **incubate** the eggs. Green turtles do not guard their nests. The eggs are in danger from animals and people who dig them up for food.

This nest was destroyed by wild animals.

Hatching

The turtles develop inside the eggs for two months. Then they are ready to hatch. They use an **egg tooth** to help break out of their shells.

A newly hatched green turtle breaks out of the nest.

The newly hatched turtles push their way through the sandy nest and onto the beach. They scurry across the beach toward the sea.

Predators

Most young turtles leave their nests at night. There are not as many **predators** around at this time. Crabs, gulls, and other animals eat newly hatched turtles.

Newly hatched green turtles enter the sea at night.

Young turtles that reach the sea are still in danger. Many fish eat young turtles. No one is sure where the turtles go after they enter the ocean.

Feeding

Young turtles are **omnivores**. They eat plants and small sea animals. Adult green turtles are **herbivores**. They eat seaweed and grasses.

Young turtles return to shallower parts of the sea when they are about 15 inches (40 centimeters) long. Only very large fish will eat them at this size.

Endangered Animals

Green turtles are **endangered**. They have fewer and fewer quiet places to breed. Many predators eat green turtles.

Gulls catch and eat young green turtles.

Probably only two turtles from a clutch of more than 100 eggs will survive. Few green turtles grow up to migrate, mate, and have young of their own. Those that do survive may live 50 years or longer.

Protecting the Green Turtle

Some beaches are kept only for breeding turtles. Scientists study green turtles on these beaches. They want to learn more about where the turtles live, how they breed, and how people can protect them.

The Life Cycle of a Green Turtle

adults mating

laying eggs

adult turtle

hatching eggs

young turtles
going to sea

Glossary

breed	to mate and produce young
clutch	a group of eggs laid at the same time in the same place
egg tooth	a sharp, hard point of skin on the tip of a hatching turtle's beak
endangered	in danger of becoming extinct
flippers	flat legs used for swimming
herbivore	an animal that feeds on plants
incubate	to keep an egg warm for a period of time while it develops
mate	to join with a breeding partner to produce young
migrate	to travel from one place to another, often covering long distances
omnivore	an animal that feeds on both plants and animals
predator	an animal that hunts other animals for food
rudder	a piece of equipment used for steering
scutes	bony plates or large scales on a turtle's shell

Index